# Gobey
## GETS FULL
### good nutrition in a nutshell™

• BY •

Judy Caplan MS, RD

• ILLUSTRATED BY •

Frances Caplan

Visit www.gobefull.com to order additional copies.

This book is dedicated to

Health Nuts everywhere.

I am Gobey the Health Nut.

I like to eat healthy food.

2

But it wasn't always this way. Like a lot of nuts I know,
I was hooked on candy, cookies, and fast food.
Chips and pretzels too.

Then one day I fell off my skateboard and cracked open my shell.

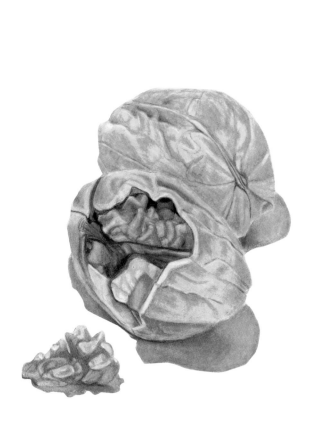
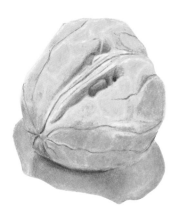

My mom pieced me back together and took me to see the Nut Doctor. After a little poking and prodding the doctor said, "Hmm, I know just what you need to help your shell heal quickly." So he sent me to a nice lady in a white coat called a nutritionist.

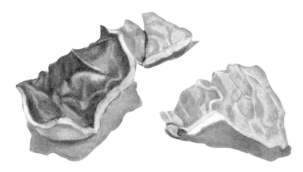

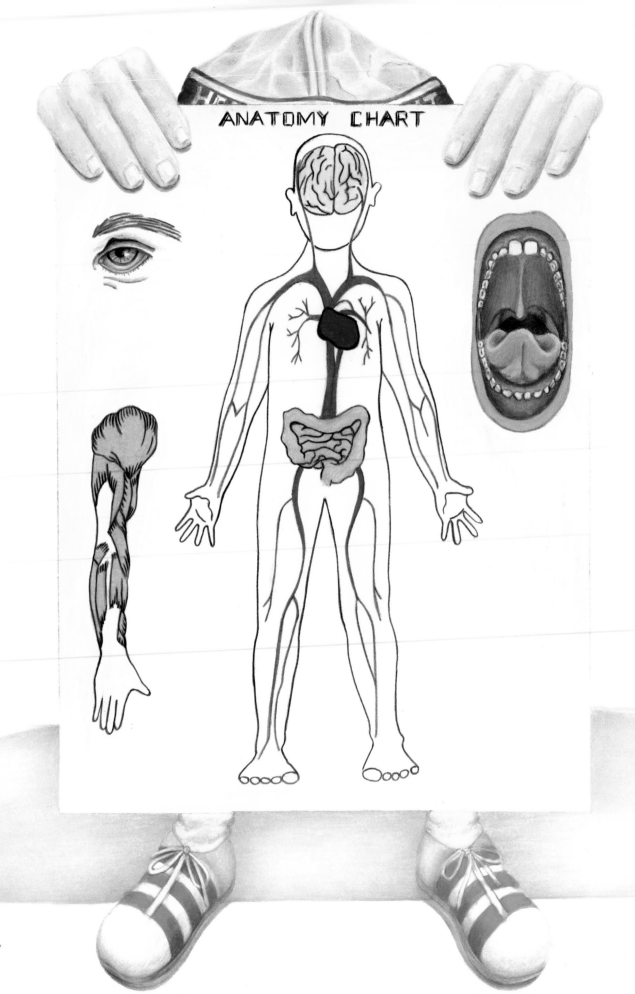

ANATOMY CHART

The nutritionist had special glasses that could see right through my shell. "Good grief Gobey," she shrieked, "your shell is filled with organs, not nuts."

The nutritionist taught me so much about how to keep fit, inside and out, that I had to make up a code word to help me remember it all. The code word is *GoBeFull*. The letters in *GoBeFull* stand for eight things I can do to be healthy and strong. Now you can *GoBeFull* and be healthy and strong like me.

**G**reens   **F**ruit

**O**live Oil   **U**nrefined Grains

**B**eans   **L**ean Protein

**E**xercise  **L**abels

# GREENS & OTHER VEGGIES

It turns out the nutritionist wasn't just nice, she was really smart. She knew just what I needed. Now I love to eat veggies. See my big eyes? The orange color in carrots helps me see in the dark. The other bright colors in veggies work magic inside my body.

Now I pile them on pizza.
Stack them on sandwiches.
Crunch them in my mouth for a crispy snack.

Can you circle the veggies you like to eat?

| | | |
|---|---|---|
| Artichokes | Cauliflower | Mushrooms |
| Asparagus | Chili peppers | Peas |
| Broccoli | Green peppers | Red peppers |
| Cabbage | Jicama | Spinach |
| Carrots (my favorite) | Lettuce | Tomatoes |

GOBEFULL

# EXERCISE

If you're like me, you like moving and grooving. Exercise keeps my brain happy and my heart strong. Fresh air is good for my lungs and sunshine strengthens my bones. Instead of skateboarding, now I play a terrific game of tether ball.

Can you put a ✓ by your favorite activities?

Baseball

Basketball

Biking

Capture the flag

Jumping rope

Karate

Kickball

Running

Scooter riding

Skating

Skipping

Soccer

Swimming

Tag

Tennis

Tether ball
(my favorite)

Walking

# FRUIT

The other day while playing hide and seek, I hid inside a giant cantaloupe. The fruit smelled so yummy that I ate my way out of the moist melon. When I finally popped through, I was wearing a banana hat!

Fruit reminds me of candy because it is so sweet and juicy. Now I eat more fruit and less candy.

Which fruits do you think are the sweetest?

| | | |
|---|---|---|
| Apple | Grapes | Peaches |
| Apricot | Kiwi | Pears |
| Berries | Mango | Persimmons |
| Cherries | Melons | Pineapple |
| Dates | Orange | Raisins |
| Figs | Papaya | Tangerines |

GOBEFULL

# UNREFINED GRAINS

When mom yells, "Slow down," I find a quiet spot to chill. I like to hollow out a warm loaf of freshly baked bread and crawl inside. I like whole wheat bread because it is brown like me.

Unrefined grains are full of fiber and a little bit scratchy. Fiber acts like a broom inside my intestines and sweeps them clean. Now I eat whole grain cereal for breakfast; no more of that sweet sugary stuff. I even ask for whole wheat crust when we order pizza to go.

Which foods will you pack in your lunch box?

Baked corn chips
Bran muffin
Corn tortilla
Oatmeal raisin cookie

Popcorn
Whole grain cereals
Whole grain pretzels
Whole grain wrap

Whole wheat bagel
Whole wheat bread
Whole wheat pizza

# LEAN PROTEIN

I like to play "restaurant." I love to cook fish because it smells up the whole house!

The nutritionist told me lean protein builds muscle and helps me grow. Now I eat lean protein every day. Lean means low in fat, like a lean mean fighting machine (that's me). Lean protein comes from both plants and animals.

Can you pick out the plant foods from the list?

Baked beans

Baked chicken

Edamame

Fat-free chocolate milk

Flank steak

Grilled fish

Low-fat string cheese

Low-fat yogurt

Roasted turkey

Salmon

Shrimp

Sushi

Tofu

GO B E F U L L

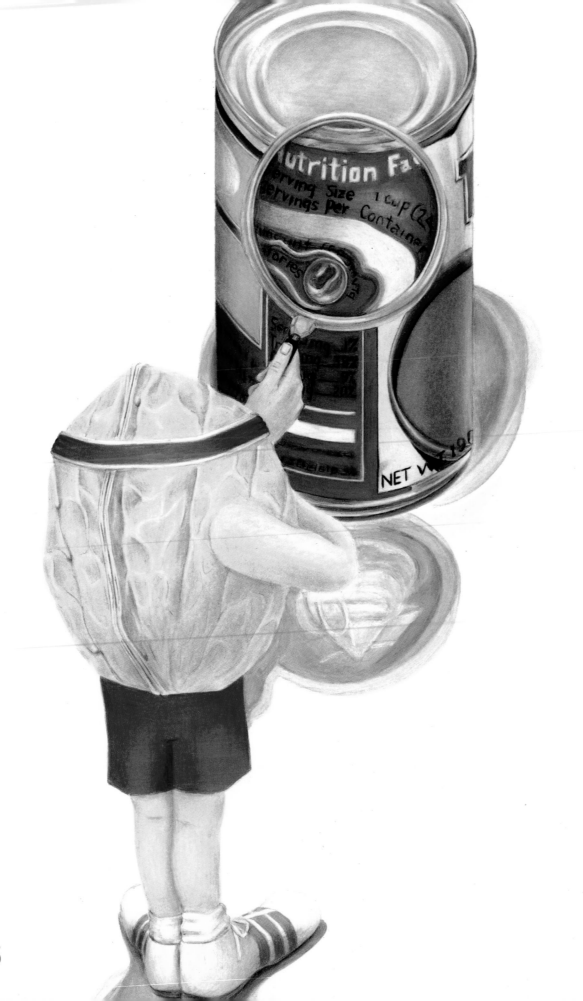

# LABELS

Thanks to the nutritionist, my shell is healed. Now I read labels to stay healthy and strong.

Labels tell me if my cookie has healthy oil.

Labels tell me if my bread is made from unrefined grains.

Labels tell me if my cereal has plenty of fiber.

Labels tell me if my protein is lean.

Labels help me GoBeFull.

*Remember*: Fresh fruit and vegetables never need labels because they are always a healthy choice.

The next time you are hungry and are thinking about what to eat, remember my simple code for good nutrition in a nutshell.

See you around,
Gobey